Little Horses

Deborah Kelly

Illustrated by
Jenni Goodman

For my Dad,
whose love of seahorses
spans 73 years

- DK -

To my wonderful free-diving
family, your love for the ocean
makes me smile.

- JG -

Little Horses

Text © Deborah Kelly, 2024
Illustrations © Jenni Goodman, 2024

Print ISBN: 978-1-76111-131-0

Published by Wombat Books, 2024
PO Box 302,
Chinchilla QLD 4413
Australia
www.wombatrhiza.com.au

A catalogue record for this
book is available from the
National Library of Australia

Little Horses

Deborah Kelly

Illustrated by
Jenni Goodman

Out in the bay, where sailboats glide
Little horses drift and hide

Changing colour so predators pass
In gardens of sponge and coral and grass

Out in the bay, to gentle waves
Little horses bend and sway

Holding on with spiral tails
To grassy wisps and coral rails

Out in the bay,
swivelling eyes

Scan the water,
spot the prize!

A nod of the head that's
lightning-quick

A slurp, a gulp! Mmm ...
tasty shrimp!

Out in the bay, now skies grow black

The wind picks up, waves peak and –

SSSSSSSSSH!

Sponges tumble
coral breaks
Little horses ...

... swept away.

Out in the bay, a whitewashed churn
Of little horses tumbles, turns

Reaching out with all their might
Two spiralled tails ...

Out in the bay, a storm has passed
The wild sea now calm at last

Weary horses bob and ride
With nothing to eat and nowhere to hide

Then
out in the bay,
in deserts blue

Swivelling eyes spot
something ...

... new!

With baby corals and young seagrass

A funny shape

that's built to last

Out in the bay, where sailboats glide
Tiny horses learn to hide

Changing colour so predators pass ...

... in gardens of sponge and coral and grass.

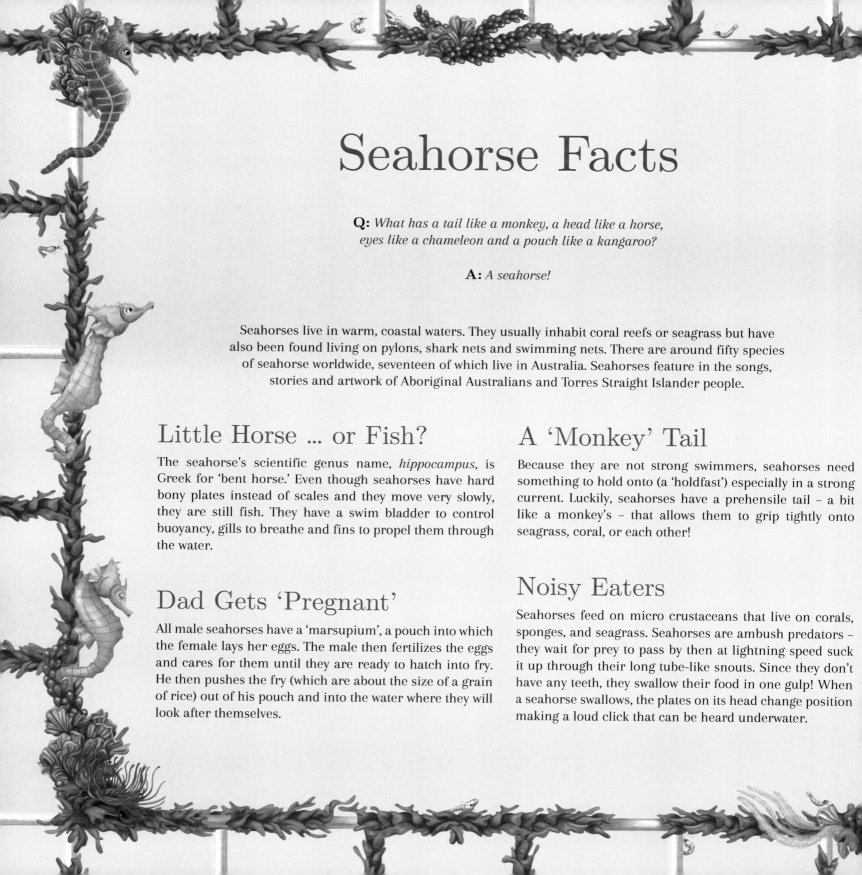

Seahorse Facts

Q: *What has a tail like a monkey, a head like a horse, eyes like a chameleon and a pouch like a kangaroo?*

A: *A seahorse!*

Seahorses live in warm, coastal waters. They usually inhabit coral reefs or seagrass but have also been found living on pylons, shark nets and swimming nets. There are around fifty species of seahorse worldwide, seventeen of which live in Australia. Seahorses feature in the songs, stories and artwork of Aboriginal Australians and Torres Straight Islander people.

Little Horse ... or Fish?

The seahorse's scientific genus name, *hippocampus*, is Greek for 'bent horse.' Even though seahorses have hard bony plates instead of scales and they move very slowly, they are still fish. They have a swim bladder to control buoyancy, gills to breathe and fins to propel them through the water.

Dad Gets 'Pregnant'

All male seahorses have a 'marsupium', a pouch into which the female lays her eggs. The male then fertilizes the eggs and cares for them until they are ready to hatch into fry. He then pushes the fry (which are about the size of a grain of rice) out of his pouch and into the water where they will look after themselves.

A 'Monkey' Tail

Because they are not strong swimmers, seahorses need something to hold onto (a 'holdfast') especially in a strong current. Luckily, seahorses have a prehensile tail – a bit like a monkey's – that allows them to grip tightly onto seagrass, coral, or each other!

Noisy Eaters

Seahorses feed on micro crustaceans that live on corals, sponges, and seagrass. Seahorses are ambush predators – they wait for prey to pass by then at lightning speed suck it up through their long tube-like snouts. Since they don't have any teeth, they swallow their food in one gulp! When a seahorse swallows, the plates on its head change position making a loud click that can be heard underwater.

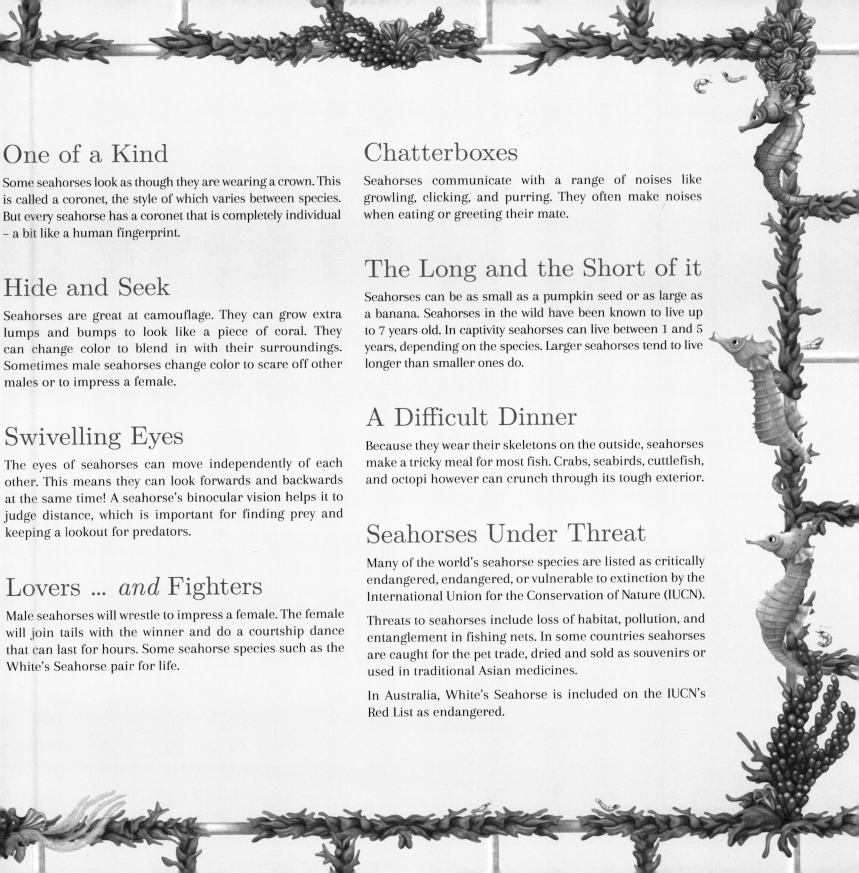

One of a Kind

Some seahorses look as though they are wearing a crown. This is called a coronet, the style of which varies between species. But every seahorse has a coronet that is completely individual – a bit like a human fingerprint.

Hide and Seek

Seahorses are great at camouflage. They can grow extra lumps and bumps to look like a piece of coral. They can change color to blend in with their surroundings. Sometimes male seahorses change color to scare off other males or to impress a female.

Swivelling Eyes

The eyes of seahorses can move independently of each other. This means they can look forwards and backwards at the same time! A seahorse's binocular vision helps it to judge distance, which is important for finding prey and keeping a lookout for predators.

Lovers ... *and* Fighters

Male seahorses will wrestle to impress a female. The female will join tails with the winner and do a courtship dance that can last for hours. Some seahorse species such as the White's Seahorse pair for life.

Chatterboxes

Seahorses communicate with a range of noises like growling, clicking, and purring. They often make noises when eating or greeting their mate.

The Long and the Short of it

Seahorses can be as small as a pumpkin seed or as large as a banana. Seahorses in the wild have been known to live up to 7 years old. In captivity seahorses can live between 1 and 5 years, depending on the species. Larger seahorses tend to live longer than smaller ones do.

A Difficult Dinner

Because they wear their skeletons on the outside, seahorses make a tricky meal for most fish. Crabs, seabirds, cuttlefish, and octopi however can crunch through its tough exterior.

Seahorses Under Threat

Many of the world's seahorse species are listed as critically endangered, endangered, or vulnerable to extinction by the International Union for the Conservation of Nature (IUCN).

Threats to seahorses include loss of habitat, pollution, and entanglement in fishing nets. In some countries seahorses are caught for the pet trade, dried and sold as souvenirs or used in traditional Asian medicines.

In Australia, White's Seahorse is included on the IUCN's Red List as endangered.

What is a Seahorse Hotel?

White's Seahorse *(Hippocampus whitei)* was once common in coral, sponge and seagrass beds along the East Coast of Australia. Its two main populations were at Port Stephens (north of Newcastle) and Sydney Harbour.

When wild storms hit Port Stephens from 2010 to 2013, much of the seahorses' fragile home was swept away or buried under sand and not many of the seahorses survived. Within five years, White's Seahorse numbers were so low that it was listed as endangered by the International Union for Conservation of Nature (IUCN).

Sometime after the storms, a marine scientist called David Harasti was scuba diving the barren sea floor when he noticed an old lobster trap. Already, tiny sponges and corals had begun to grow on it. Living on the sponges and corals were tiny critters and feeding on the critters was a pair of White's Seahorses!

David had an idea. What if he made more 'lobster traps' and left them on the sea floor? They might become overgrown with coral, algae and sponges, too. They could provide a safe place full of food for the remaining White's Seahorses to hold onto and hide from predators. It could be a bit like a hotel for the White's Seahorses – a place to stay until their natural environment recovered. It might give them a chance to meet other seahorses, too.

Seahorse Hotels Project

In 2018 David built the very first seahorse hotel. He modelled it on the lobster trap that had given him the idea. He made a metal frame covered in chicken wire that was three feet long and three feet wide. It looked a bit like a cage, but the seahorses would easily be able to swim in and out.

'If we build it, they will come.'

– DAVID HARASTI

David's idea worked! Within a few months, seahorses moved into the seahorse hotels and began to breed. He made more seahorse hotels and the numbers of White's seahorse in Port Stephens began to rise.

David's seahorse hotel idea was so successful in Port Stephens that he decided to try it in Sydney Harbour, another important population of White's Seahorse. Again, the hotels worked their magic!

Inspiring Others

Other countries (Greece, the Philippines and Indonesia) soon heard about the success of David's seahorse hotels and began making their own designs with different materials, in the hope of boosting their own seahorse populations.

Into the Future

With the help of Sydney Sea Life Aquarium's seahorse captive-breeding program and the University of Technology Sydney, David's Harasti's seahorse hotels are bringing an endangered seahorse back from the brink of extinction – and inspiring other countries to do the same.